THE BRUSSELS CONVENTION
AND FREE TRADE.

SPEECHES DELIVERED BY

EARL SPENCER, K.G.,

AND

SIR H. CAMPBELL-BANNERMAN, M.P.,

*At a Cobden Club Banquet, on
Nov. 28th, 1902.*

CASSELL AND COMPANY, LIMITED:
LONDON, PARIS, NEW YORK & MELBOURNE.
1903.

In the interest of creating a more extensive selection of rare historical book reprints, we have chosen to reproduce this title even though it may possibly have occasional imperfections such as missing and blurred pages, missing text, poor pictures, markings, dark backgrounds and other reproduction issues beyond our control. Because this work is culturally important, we have made it available as a part of our commitment to protecting, preserving and promoting the world's literature. Thank you for your understanding.

THE BRUSSELS CONVENTION AND FREE TRADE.

LORD SPENCER'S SPEECH.

Lord Spencer proposed " Prosperity to the Cobden Club." In doing so he said :—

Twenty-two years ago, when I had the privilege of occupying the chair as I do to-night, I was fresh in the second Cabinet of Mr. Gladstone. I was asked to preside at the Cobden Club dinner, which took place in those days at Greenwich. Those were not the days when Cabinet Ministers and Members of Parliament made a hasty rush out of London for the week-end holiday. (Laughter and cheers.) I am not saying a word against the week-end holiday ; but am only referring to what was the practice in those days. Mr. Gladstone used to have Cabinets on a Saturday, and on the occasion to which I refer I met at the Cabinet one who was always most kind to me—a very great man, whose name I am sure will always be received with enthusiasm, not only in Liberal circles but especially in Cobden Club circles—I mean Mr. Bright. (Cheers.) I told Mr. Bright I should have to leave early that afternoon. Mr. Bright inquired the reason. I replied, "Oh, for my sins"—and you must recollect that I disliked speaking then even more than I dislike speaking now—"for my sins I have to go down to Greenwich to preside over the Cobden Club dinner." Mr. Bright turned to me gravely but kindly and said, "Lord Spencer, you ought not to use expressions like that, for a greater honour could not be conferred on anyone than that of presiding at a Cobden Club dinner." (Cheers.) That great man, whom we all revere now as we revered him then, then gave in a sort of way his blessing to these dinners. (Cheers.)

THE WORK OF SIR ROBERT PEEL.

It is not necessary for me to go at length into the principles and objects with which the Cobden Club was founded, but I often think that the younger politicians, unless they have studied very carefully their political history, may sometimes hesitate about Free Trade principles, or not know why the Cobden Club was founded to maintain them. It is on that account that gatherings like this are very useful, for they explain the origin of the Cobden Club and why Free Trade holds such a high place even now in the policy of this country. People sometimes forget the state of things which existed in this country before the days of Free Trade. (Cheers.) A terrible state of things existed. Agricultural depression was of a deeper and worse character than now. There was a cessation of work in the great commercial centres, rioting bordering on revolution was going on, and to many minds it appeared that the country was verging on a state of bankruptcy. Sir Robert Peel, by his vigorous application of the policy of Free Trade, overcame those evils and put the country on a more stable and satisfactory basis. It was on Free Trade principles that our great commerce throughout the world was established and the great riches in our manufacturing centres were collected. Without Free Trade we should not have had this great amelioration of the state of the people, this great increase of our trade which has made us the greatest trading nation in the world, and not only a great trading nation, but also a nation who is spreading her noble and high principles of liberty and civilisation by means of her trade in every quarter of the globe. (Cheers.) This great change is due almost entirely to the principle of Free Trade. And it is not only Sir Robert Peel that we have to thank for Free Trade, but other great men. There were Cobden, Bright, and Villiers, and last, but not least, our great leader, Mr. Gladstone—(cheers)—who all fought and worked for that great principle and helped to build up that satisfactory edifice of prosperity all over the world of which we are so proud. (Cheers.)

MR. CHAMBERLAIN'S RECENT SPEECH.

We have had great discussions on this subject recently, and I have noticed particularly that those who are bringing forward measures to which Free

Traders have the strongest possible dislike, because they break their cherished principles, constantly assert that they are true Free Traders. Their Protectionism sneaks out though sometimes, and in the speeches that they have made in the House of Commons there are doctrines which show what the beginning would end in if they had their way. There was a speech of Mr. Chamberlain's the other day—I do not suppose I need have any scruple about quoting him, though at this moment he may be tossing in a very disagreeable place. (Laughter.) He avowed himself a very strong Free Trader; but he could not help letting the cat out of the bag. He said in that speech: "I do not believe for a moment that there are more than 50,000 people employed in different trades which in any sensible degree are dependent on sugar; but whether they be 50,000 or 1,000,000, I say there is nothing whatever to induce us to believe that we might not have had even more British subjects, more British capital, more British machinery in sugar refinery and production if only we had protected them against this competition in time." Is this Free Trade? Are these the doctrines of a Free Trader? I say they are the doctrines of a Protectionist. (Cheers.) Before I touch on the subject of sugar I should like to point to another danger which accompanies this praise of Empire which is being sung so often in triumphant tones by so many Jingoes and others. I am not at all one who wishes to underrate the Empire. I wish that we should do our duty towards the Empire and to our Colonies, and try to bind them together in the closest bonds to us, but I think a great deal too much has been said on that subject. I fear that too often there is a danger of our sacrificing the greater interests of our trade with the world to the smaller interest that belongs to trade, imports and exports, with our Colonies.

THE NAVIGATION LAWS.

I feel this very strongly. At the conference of Premiers which was held during the year there was one very remarkable resolution which was passed, which I think is another indication that we all, as Cobdenites, should try to prevent the spread of fatal and wrong principles—fatal and wrong action as regards the great principles of Free Trade. The resolution was:

"That it is desirable that the attention of the Governments of the Colonies and the United Kingdom should be called to the present state of the navigation laws in the Empire and in other countries, and to the advisability of refusing the privileges of coastwise trade, including trade between the mother country and its colonies and possessions, and between one colony or possession and another, to countries in which the corresponding trade is confined to ships of their own nationality, and also to the laws affecting shipping, with a view of seeing whether any other steps should be taken to promote Imperial trade in British vessels."

Is not that going back to the old navigation laws? Since 1854, when they were finally repealed, our coastwise trade has increased by leaps and bounds, and what share do you think the dangerous foreigner has in that trade? His share in our coastwise traffic is only 0·4 per cent. (Laughter.) Are we going back to those navigation laws? I say that as Free Traders we must protest against it.

THE BRUSSELS CONVENTION.

With regard to the Brussels Convention, I am not in favour of bounties, for they are not in accordance with Free Trade principles. I do not at all object to our neighbours giving up bounties, if they do so freely, and unshackled by conditions; but in the circumstances in which the Brussels Convention has been agreed to I maintain that we shall be doing a very great injustice, an unnecessary injustice, to a very large body of consumers in this country. (Cheers.) Why is it done? It is done, as we were told, in order to save the West Indies from ruin. Yet there are many people who say that even if bounties are abolished the sugar producers in these colonies will not be able to hold their heads above water. There is a very remarkable passage in a despatch from Sir H. M. Jackson, Governor of the Leeward Islands, to Mr. Chamberlain on this question of the bounties. He writes:

"What the effect of the abolition of bounties may prove to be in large colonies producing high-grade sugars it is not for me to say, since the Leeward Islands are not among them; but it is only too certain that in these islands producing only Muscovado, and that by means of indifferent machinery, the immediate effect will be the reverse of beneficial. The American market is now the only one, a precarious one at best, but still the only one now open to the low-grade sugars of these islands, and immediately the bounties are abolished that market will be thrown open to the competition of the whole of the Continental beet sugars. That thriving industry, thanks to years of artificial stimulus, is well equipped with the most modern machinery, while the planters of Antigua who have had to face year after year of serious and increasing loss, are wholly without the means of obtaining capital to improve their old-fashioned and wasteful process. . . . It is also absolutely certain, as shown by Dr. Morris, that directly the Muscovado and beet sugars come into open competition in the same markets, as they must do on the abolition of bounties, the former trade must be annihilated unless the production can be improved."

We find this evidence from a Governor who evidently understands the subject in his island, and the same argument applies to every West Indian island producing low-grade sugar that, directly the bounties are removed, and there is free and open competition between the beetroot sugar and the low-grade West Indian sugar, the latter must go to the wall.

*

BEET SUGAR AND CANE SUGAR.

There are some very interesting figures in an American publication presented to Parliament which show very clearly that for some years past there has been a most tremendous struggle between cane sugar and beetroot sugar. It is the tropics fighting against the temperate zone, and the curious thing is that the increase in the beetroot sugar is far larger than the increase in the cane sugar, though the latter has also increased.

"Thus to compare but the middle of the last century with its close, it is found that the total production of sugar increased from above 1,500,000 tons to about 8,500,000, or over 5½ times. Of this increase by far the larger share is due to the growth of beet sugar production, which, practically beginning about the middle of the century (with a production of about 200,000 tons in all), showed at the end of the century a total product of 5,500,000 tons."

These are very remarkable figures, and show what the increase of beetroot sugar has done towards lowering the price of sugar. I want very much to know whether, even if it is right to say that the price of sugar will rise, these West Indian sugar growers will be able to compete in the open market. At present their great market is in the United States. Four-fifths, I think, of their sugar goes to the United States. At present they have the benefit of the countervailing duties which the

Americans have against bounty-grown sugar. Under the Brussels Convention that benefit will disappear, and they will have to compete on perfectly even terms with all the sugar of the world.

COUNTERVAILING DUTIES.

The force of the Convention rests entirely on the point that under certain circumstances each country which is a party to the Convention must have countervailing duties against any country where bounties exist. I, for one, maintain that no one who has the slightest feeling with regard to Free Trade can say that the establishment of countervailing duties can be in accord with those great principles of which we are so proud. If countervailing duties are established we shall not only have a war of tariffs—I see in the speeches in the House on the Government side that they have ridiculed that — but we shall traverse one of the most important diplomatic arrangements which we have, for these countervailing duties will do away with the most-favoured-nation clauses in our commercial treaties. But that is not the only objection. How are these countervailing duties to be fixed? They are to be settled by an international tribunal not named by us, and upon which we shall only have one commissioner. All the other nine Governments who are parties to the Convention will each have their nominee. The body thus constituted has to decide the question whether any country has a bounty or an equivalent of a bounty, and if they come to the conclusion that that country has a bounty, then the countries who are parties to the convention are bound by the Convention to impose countervailing duties against that country. Was there ever before such a proposal as this—that the taxation of this country shall practically be left in the hands of a foreign body not named by us, and on which we only have one representative?

TAXED BY A FOREIGN COMMISSION.

I do not know what may happen in the House of Commons; but it seems to me an infringement of the rights of that body if the taxation of the country is practically taken out of our hands, as it will be if we agree to the passing of this Convention. (Cheers.) A more monstrous, a more radical change in all the best constitutional doctrines we have ever held could not have been framed than that which places the settlement of these countervailing duties in the hands of this foreign body. (Cheers.) I must apologise for having dwelt so long on this subject. It seems to me that all Free Traders and all who revere the great names of those who worked for Free Trade, must be up and doing. They must protest with all their might against this great injustice—this favour and privilege of the few to the prejudice of the many. (Cheers.) It has been well said, "We have liberty to speak as we like, we have liberty to act as we like; give us liberty to buy and sell as we like." (Cheers.) Do not for a moment be led astray by those who say they are acting under Free Trade principles. No one can contend that countervailing duties or the total prohibition of articles of necessity to the people are in accordance with Free Trade. (Cheers.) The authors of this Convention may take action under the mask, falsely assumed, of Free Trade, but they may depend upon it their mask will be rudely torn off and the mean and hateful figure of Protection will appear. That figure, which nearly ruined this country in the early part of the nineteenth century, may yet, if allowed to rule our policy, ruin our future prosperity and bring disaster and financial confusion in its wake to our producers, manufacturers, and consumers. (Loud cheers.)

In conclusion, I urge you to fight strenuously to maintain the right of the forty millions who inhabit the United Kingdom and who pay the cost of the Empire, to buy their goods in the cheapest market, unhindered by laws devised for the protection of privileged classes and "privileged interests."

SIR H. CAMPBELL-BANNERMAN'S SPEECH.

Sir Henry Campbell-Bannerman, on rising to respond, was greeted with enthusiasm. He said:

Lord Spencer, Ladies and Gentlemen,—I feel highly honoured in being called upon to respond for this toast, and I beg to assure you that there is no toast that would have come nearer to my innermost sympathies. There must be some besides my noble friend and myself here present—though I fear that the lapse of years may have made them a minority in this company—whose thoughts go back, as mine instinctively do, to the old days, the golden days of the Cobden Club dinners, when we, the members of the Club, met, not as to-night for the purpose of bracing ourselves and stimulating each other for the defence of our essential principles, but for the perhaps pleasanter purpose of triumphing in the acceptance by the country of these principles—a triumph which we believed to be permanent and irrevocable in the minds and feelings and judgment of our countrymen. (Cheers.) I well remember the pleasant sail down the River Thames under the genial tutelage of Mr. Thomas Bayley Potter, and the jocund banquet at the Ship Tavern at Greenwich, and the speeches—the not too long speeches—(a laugh)—which were devoted not so much to vaunting the excellence of our principles as to celebrating their embodiment, as we thought, for ever in the public policy of the country. (Cheers.) Who would have thought then that our own generation would see a British Government making inroad after inroad upon those principles— upon the principles which we then believed, and we now believe as strongly as ever, are the basis of British prosperity? (Cheers.) Our confidence continued, ladies and gentlemen, until very recent years. The truth is that the very strength of the Free Trade position is a large source of weakness. No one imagined that the position would ever be seriously assailed. Here have been years upon years of prosperity such as was not dreamt of fifty, forty, or even thirty years ago, and in the midst of this full-blooded strength and health the constituted physician, I was going to say, without the consent of the patient, but certainly without his full appreciation of what is happening, steps in and orders a change of diet, and puts him upon a reducing regimen, altering the very diet and regimen to which the abounding health is owing. (Laughter and cheers.)

FISCAL RETROGRESSION.

The country may well be slow to believe it, but the country does not realise the retrogression which, not in fiscal matters alone, is going on step by step under our very eyes. (Cheers.) Ever since the Reform Act was passed, and the main political energies of the nation were devoted to the abolishment of privileges and tests, and to the breaking down of restraints upon trade, it had come to be assumed among us that everything we gained in this movement of emancipation would be secured without any serious effort. The work of Peel and Cobden and Gladstone we accepted—in spite of the little murmurs and fumes and frets of a few people—we accepted them as part of the national heritage, and we all hoped that the policy of the country would go on in conformity with the principles which it had cost so much to establish, and which had been tested and tried with such marvellous and startlingly successful results. But there are two classes of Free Traders. There is the Free Trader active and the Free Trader passive. To the category of active Free Traders let us hope all the members of the Cobden Club belong. (Hear, hear.) The passive Free Traders are the great mass of our countrymen who have prospered under the system without fully realising how much they owe to it. (Cheers.) They have been like M. Jourdain, who had been talking prose all his life without knowing it. (Laughter.) The men of the existing generation have never felt the pinch which was felt by the men of the old generation. They have never experienced in themselves or witnessed in others those terrible conditions of life to which my noble friend has referred, which prevailed both in town and country, and which forced Sir Robert Peel and his friends to throw prejudices—aye, and in some cases even pledges—to the winds in order to mitigate evils so appalling. They know nothing of the misery and suffering, of the discontent, of the social disorder, which attended and were induced by the old protective laws. (Hear, hear.) They have enjoyed stability in trade and commerce, financial stability, political stability—(hear, hear)—high wages, cheap commodities, to a degree that no generation before them ever attained. (Cheers.) They are vaguely aware that this is nominally a Free Trade country, and that it must be all right ; but when a particular trade clamours for its own particular protection they not unnaturally think that the poor fellows are not unreasonable in trying to protect their own interests, and they may regard as altogether extravagant the views of those of us who see in any breaking down of the barrier of impartial freedom a letting in of the waters. (Cheers.) Now, at the present time I think I am right in saying that it is not the open hostility of the avowed Protectionist that we have to combat. The Protectionist, indeed, no longer speaks with the bated breath that we were accustomed to, but he is still apologetic in his manner, and he shrinks from exposing to the country in all its beauty—(laughter)—his full theory lest the country should be startled and alarmed. Even when he sets about a smashing blow against the keystone of the arch of Free Trade or lays a silent mine under the corner-stone of that edifice, he does it in Free Trade clothes —(laughter)—and he tries to show, as we have seen not very long ago, that Protection after all is the only practical way of acting upon Free Trade principles. (Laughter and cheers.)

DANGERS OF INDIFFERENCE.

It is not of these, ladies and gentlemen, that we have most reason to be afraid. Their inconsistency, their absurdity, their selfish interest, it may be, is only too apparent. (Hear, hear.) No; it is in the ill-informed indifference of the average man that the danger lies. (Hear, hear.) He is a good fellow. He is well off. He does not go below the surface of things. He is easy-going and good-hearted. He is easily caught by a fallacy which appeals to his sympathy. The special duty and function of this Club, my lords, ladies, and gentlemen, my lords especially—(laughter)—we always look to them for an example, and we don't look in vain to the sort of lords we have here—(cheers)—the special duty and function of this Club is to open this man's eyes to the real issues involved in small and apparently technical questions, to explain the root principles upon which our established national policy is founded, and, using the old weapons of appeal to the lessons of history, to common sense, and reason and humanity, and adding to our armoury the additional weapon furnished by the practical experience of the last half century—it is to reaffirm and re-confirm the adherence of the nation to the essential vital policy of freedom. This I take to be the object of this dinner. (Cheers.) It is not for that old purpose to which I have referred—the honourable and creditable purpose of congratulating ourselves upon our position, it is not that we may pat each other on the back that we are here, but that we may smite ourselves on the chest and resolve that we will do each of us what we can, to the best of our power, to secure in perpetuity to our country the blessings which for half a century we have enjoyed. (Cheers.) And what a moment it is at which, as it happens, we are meeting. If I may refer to a personal recollection, I remember when I was a boy—it was very improper—but I was being instructed in the elements of religion in my own home—(laughter)—it was very wrong—(renewed laughter)—instead of having it conducted, as we were told last night ought to be done, by an anointed clergyman—(laughter)—and one of the books that was most familiar to me then was a book which was called "Undesigned Coincidences." What those were I cannot at this distance of time tax my memory to recollect, but it was surely something intended to "justify the ways of God to man."

THE CLOVEN FOOT.

But the words came into my head—"undesigned coincidences." When this meeting of the Cobden Club was fixed, Lord Welby, many weeks ago, between you and me, for the 28th November, little did we think what would happen in the House of Commons on the 24th November. In the very week in which we are meeting extraordinary occurrences have happened in that great Chamber. Why, sir, Monday last did more for us than a dozen banquets or a hundred leaflets. Never has the cloven foot been popped out so far beyond the ambit of the crural integument. (Laughter.) It is true that we were not unprepared. My experience of doctors is that when they are going to give you a strong drug, they generally a day or two before give you some other drug to prepare the way for the strong drug. And so for the last two or three years we have had little taxes imposed, it may have been, in anticipation of this greater effort. They were taxes of a most questionable kind. Lord Spencer has referred to them, but I venture to go over them again. They were all of the same character. To begin with, they were all suspiciously and mysteriously innocuous. No one has to pay them. There was the sugar duty. It was to fall entirely on the producer. (Laughter.) Then we had the coal export duty, which was to be paid wholly by the consumer. (Laughter.) Then we had the corn duty. That was still more marvellous, because, in the course of its career, from the man who grew to the man who ate, passing through the hands of the carrier and the shipper to the merchant and the miller, and the baker and the retailer, this tax, like the commodity with which it was associated, was to be triturated to such a degree that one puff from the mouth of the Chancellor of the Exchequer would scatter it into thin air. (Laughter.) These taxes were to be such that nobody would feel them.

"PAINLESS TAXATION."

I go along the street, or I look at the outside—mostly the outside—of a magazine occasionally, and I see there is such a thing as painless dentistry. This painless taxation is to be extracted from the pocket of the taxpayer and he is not to feel it in any sense except perhaps a pleasurable sensation. (Laughter.) But that was not the most remarkable circumstance. The most remarkable circumstance was that everybody concerned, from the First Lord of the Treasury down through his colleagues, including, of course, the Chancellor of the Exchequer, would not one of them have touched any of these taxes with the tip of their finger if there had been any flavour whatever of Protection about them. (Laughter.) Such is the homage that political vice pays to political virtue. (Loud cheers.) Why, we all knew at the time, every man with an ounce of brains in his head and with any acuteness whatever knew, that they were Protection *pro tanto* so far as they operated, Protection and nothing else. (Hear, hear.) But on Monday there was no disguise; and the country, so far as the Government can compass it, stands now publicly committed to a deliberate sanction of full-blooded and pugnacious Protection. (Hear, hear.) Now, on Monday last, I want to ask, where was our old friend the ex-Chancellor of the Exchequer? (Hear, hear.) He has been our sheet-anchor all this time. We took him at his own estimate, which was in point of financial and fiscal virtue and valour a very high estimate. (Hear, hear.) Where was he? He has ceased to be in the Government, but he is still, I believe, a member of the House of Commons.

(Hear, hear.) The present Chancellor of the Exchequer was indeed present. He is a man for whom I have a great personal respect, and in whom I have considerable personal belief. But I would say this of him in these fiscal matters, that he reminds me of what the French say of a père de famille: "Il est capable de tout." (Laughter and "Hear, hear.") But what a solace to our distressed minds it would have been if we had had from the Chancellor of the Exchequer one of those admirable little homilies on sound doctrine and his usual assurance of sterling fidelity to it to which we have been accustomed. Our minds are full of this question of the Brussels Convention. I can add really nothing to the very full and accurate analysis that you, Lord Spencer, have given of the question. After-dinner speakers ought to recollect that their audience are busy digesting their dinners, and I can imagine nothing less conducive to healthful digestion than a yard of dry argument, garnished with a hatful of statistics. I will, therefore, not harass you with them.

THE CONVENTION IS PROTECTION.

But this Convention is Protection, and nothing less. Who can doubt it? Oh, but they say, "It abolishes bounties, and this is Free Trade." It does not abolish bounties. (Hear, hear.) On the contrary, it abolishes part of the bounties, but it confirms and sanctions and perpetuates the rest. Notice the position of the three countries, Italy, Spain, Sweden, they are betwixt and between—they are not in the full tide of the agreement, but they are not left outside altogether. They are allowed to go on imposing their bounties, provided they do not export the sugar. That is to say, they make up for one breach of true economic law by imposing another breach. I do not take much comfort from that. And then bounty-fed sugar may be bad; but what about tariff-fed sugar? Tariff-fed sugar is, if anything, worse. And the tariff remains; and the surtax remains. (Hear, hear.) It not only remains, but we associate ourselves with the system. Let me read the words of the protocol of this precious Convention. Now, these words are not the words of some outlandish doctrinaire or misguided and ill-informed country. They are the language of the British people through their representatives. "The object of the surtax," says the protocol, "is the efficacious protection of the market of each producing country." And then they go on to say, "The high contracting parties reserve to themselves the right, each one as concerns itself, to propose an increase of the surtax should considerable quantities of sugar"—just imagine such an awful thing happening—(laughter)—"from one of the contracting States find their way into their territories." So we are declaring that it is an abominable thing, which should be prevented by any means, that the surplus "considerable quantities of sugar" from one State should find its way into the territories of another. (Laughter.) This is the sentiment of the British Government as expressed in the protocol. This was the honest interpretation of it by Baron von Thielmann in the Reichstag in Berlin: "The surtax —it might be a trifle higher—is amply sufficient to protect our home production of sugar against an importation of it from neighbouring countries." This is the sort of thing to which this Free Trade country is made a party in this year of our Lord 1902. And then, the surtax remaining, you have the cartels and the trusts and all the other arrangements which depend upon the surtax for their full efficiency left in their native vigour, but with the greater influence which is given to them by the express sanction of the Free Trade Government of Great Britain. (Cheers.) Remember in looking at these things the essential difference between us and the other parties to this Convention. In the first place, these Powers with which we are dealing are our rivals. They differ from us in almost every particular. They are producers.

THE TWO SIDES OF THE FENCE.

We, excepting the West Indies, may be called the consumers. We are the largest consumers— certainly in Europe, at any rate, and therefore our interest is not identical with theirs, or even commensurate with theirs. Again, we are a Free Trade country, we profess our belief in free imports, and in leaving trade and industry, whether domestic or international, to follow its natural course. (Cheers.) The other nations are all on the other side of the fence. They believe in restraint, in prohibition, in interference, in monopoly, in the aggrandisement of one particular trade at the cost of the general community, and in the diversion of the industrial energy of their people into such a channel as the statesmen of the country may wisely direct. And here we are, therefore, before the world—the protagonists of freedom, bowing the head in the temple of Rimmon, and worshipping, by our approval, gods whom, by all our traditions and professions and our real beliefs, we are bound to regard as false gods. (Cheers.) That is the nature of the Convention. We might not, of course, be able to prevent the continuance of these things. But we do more than fail to prevent them. We approve them. We give them our sanction. But it does not stop there. As my noble friend said, we promise to take retaliatory measures against the dissenting countries who do not come into the Convention—(cheers)—Nonconformists, if I may call them so—(laughter and cheers)—who are perfectly entitled to their Nonconformity. But we are so horribly orthodox that we promise to take retaliatory measures—we promise to impose countervailing duties on them, and actually to close our ports against their bounty-fed sugar; and we recognise the right of other nations to do the same. But I am told, "You need not mind that—you know that is only a threat—it will never be put into operation—it is only a threat."

"THE OPEN DOOR."

Well, I thought we were the country of the open door. But, if I have an open door and I let in A and B and C, and proceed when X, Y, and Z present themselves to say, "Hullo! Oh, you don't come in here. You must pay a heavy fine if you do. Or never mind about the fine, that is inconvenient to me—I will slam the door in your face, and bolt and bar it." And we are told that because we make that arrangement beforehand, and prevent them from attempting to come in, therefore no harm has been done—the most original idea of an open door that I have ever heard. (Laughter and cheers.) And what is the constitutional bearing of these stipulations? Again, I follow my right hon. friend, and if you hear the same thing from me that you have heard from him it is because you have committed the great mistake of asking two of us to speak on the same subject—it is not our fault. The bearing of these stipulations is perfectly monstrous, as he said—it means that we abandon our fiscal independence together with our Free Trade ways—that we subside into the tenth part of a foreign *Vehmgericht*, which is to direct us what sugar is to be countervailed, at what rate per cent. we are to countervail it, how much is to be put on for the bounty, and how much for the tariff being in excess of the Convention tariff. And this being the established order of things, the British Chancellor of the Exchequer obeys the orders that he receives from this foreign Convention, in which the Britisher is only one out of ten, and the House of Commons humbly submits to the whole transaction. ("Shame.") Sir, of all the insane schemes ever offered to a free country as a boon this is surely the maddest. (Cheers.) I trust that we shall hear a great deal more about this Convention. I have spoken of its disastrous effect upon our policy, and of its humiliating effect upon the free power of action of our country, and the dignity of our country. These are most mischievous and humiliating.

A HEAVY BLOW AT INDUSTRY.

But what shall we say when we turn to the other side of the picture? We find that while all this charming proceeding will impose upon the consumer in this country a great burden, or at any rate—I do not like to be a prophet—the risk of a great burden —upon the consumer, did I say?—yes, and upon the most dependent and indigent among the consumers —and will also infallibly strike a heavy blow against prosperous industries; at the same time it is not even claimed for it that it will have the effect of setting the West Indies on their feet. (Cheers.) What did the Colonial Secretary say about the West Indies? He said it will do three things: It will benefit the

West Indies by getting rid of the sense of injustice which presses upon them. (Laughter.) Secondly, they will get rid of the irregularity of their trade. Thirdly, it will restore their credit so that they may obtain new machinery and develop their industry—rather vague benefits to be purchased at the risk of this loss or danger of loss. I will not examine whether there is any force in the three suppositions. We are all very willing to relieve our Colonies. We all sympathise with the West Indies in their distress, but could it not be done at some less cost? (Hear, hear.) There is not only a heavy charge upon this country, but there is the renunciation of our constitutional right and the abnegation of our traditional policy. (Hear, hear.) Now consider for a moment, how does this matter stand? Before the ratification of the treaty it was necessary to obtain the assent of Parliament. I never venture to inquire into, much less to interfere with, the proceedings of the Upper House of Parliament. I do not know whether their approval has been received or not. I rather think they have never heard of it at all. The noble lord who represents the Government in that House has apparently not been aware that this treaty was under consideration. At all events, I have seen nothing in the papers to indicate that the House of Lords is going to be consulted about it. But the House of Commons has been consulted, it will be said. Yes; but has it really given its approval? One night only was allowed for the discussion—(hear, hear)—and then our tongue was tied by closure. Through the night, and up to the very end, groups of members on each side were rising to speak. I have no doubt that those members who are around me here were among those who were bobbing up and down in the course of the evening. It was well known that many of those members who rose on the Government side were rising for the purpose of expressing their disapproval of the policy of the Government. The Government had a majority of 87. The Government supporters absent and unaccounted for were 110, and the Irish Opposition was away. Which way would the Irish Opposition have voted had it been there? None of us know, especially in these days. (Laughter.) But the Irish Opposition opposed strongly every one of the taxes that put these heavy burdens upon the people. The Irish Opposition I put at a very moderate figure, at 70. If you take 70 from 87, you have not what you would call a triumphant approval by the House of Commons, in a Chamber where the Government has a normal majority of 130, of this great instrument which is to found such a monstrous new departure. Therefore, I say that we are free to renew our protest on every occasion—(loud cheers)—and I trust that this Club will not spare its efforts to strengthen our hands. (Hear, hear.)

THE RING FENCE.

Now, my lords and ladies and gentlemen, there

are two taunts that are often directed against us Free Traders, and especially against that obnoxious body, the Cobden Club. The first is that we care only for cheapness, and nothing else. The next is that we care more for the interests of other countries than our own. Need I say there is no ground whatever for these assertions? This policy of Free Trade was adopted not in the interests of other countries, but as a necessity for our country; it was adopted and is maintained and is justified in the interests of this country alone. It is, in fact, essential to our position in the world and the conditions attaching to that position, and it has been established by our experience of incalculable blessings. Why, by everything that segregates this country from the rest of the world we are injured, and ruin would come to our country if we were put in the ring fence that some people wish to see built around us. (Hear, hear.) But now there is some idea in this twentieth century of making the ring fence wider. It is no longer to be a nation that is to be self-sustaining; it is to be an empire which has to be staked off and guarded. This is a new conception, and in order to accomplish this the scheme is to be supported by preferential duties. In fact, what we are to have is a Chinese Empire, surrounded by a Chinese wall, to keep the outer barbarian at a proper and, let us hope, respectful distance. (Laughter.) Why, ladies and gentlemen, such a scheme is only visionary and wholly impracticable and wholly mischievous. It would bring ruin to our trade, the greater part of which is with foreign countries; and, lastly, by introducing into our relations with our Colonies, happily now so serene and cordial, elements of friction and jealousy and disagreement, it might be fatal to continued concord, and thus defeat that very solidarity which it was thought it would serve. (Hear, hear.) And it is by no means the smallest part of the objections to the recent breaches in our system that they invite and provoke —and are we sure that they were not intended to invite and provoke?—efforts in this dangerous direction. (Hear, hear.)

FREE TRADE, PEACE, AND GOODWILL.

Now, ladies and gentlemen, I have detained you too long, but I have been speaking entirely in answer to the toast you have proposed, which is the toast of Free Trade—Free Trade and its effect on national comfort and national prosperity. But this does not sum up the whole matter. There are other and higher purposes in view. Look at the motto of our club. On the outside of your publications there is stamped not only the "Cobden Club," not only "Free Trade," but "Free Trade, Peace, Goodwill among Nations." (Cheers.) Amid all our controversies over tariffs and protections and prohibitions let us bear in mind that these are something more than agencies for making commodities dearer, or even for diverting trade from its natural channel. They are the instruments of international cupidity, hostility, and jealousy. They are the expression of one of the most diabolically mischievous conceptions that ever entered into the mind of man or nation, viz. that we are injured when our neighbour prospers. True political and fiscal doctrine, not less than Christian doctrine, preaches the solidarity of national interests, and if we of this Club seek to break down artificial barriers between nations it is in the sacred cause of peace and goodwill. On a memorable occasion that we all remember it was said that the greatest European interest is peace. (Hear, hear.) I would go further and say that the greatest world interest is peace. (Cheers.) But looking around us on the nations of the world what do you see? You see them struggling and groaning because they are caught in an inexorable chain. It is a vicious circle. Tariffs engender jealousies, bitternesses, and quarrels. Quarrels grow into wars or necessitate crushing armaments in order to stave off wars. Armaments and wars swell expenditure. Expenditure must be met by tariffs. And so it goes on—I won't say the merry round—but the hideous and detestable round goes on. At what point in this infernal circle can you hope with any success to insert your magic wand, and stop the deadly current? Surely at the point of tariffs—(cheers)—and there alone; and it will always be the pride and glory of the order of thought which this Club, feebly it may be, and imperfectly, but still honestly, represents, that it has steadily and consistently proclaimed that policy which is the only sure avenue to peace. (Cheers.)

Printed by Libri Plureos GmbH in Hamburg, Germany